FAIRY TALE MAZES

Suzanne Ross

DOVER PUBLICATIONS, INC.
Mineola, New York

Bibliographical Note

Fairy Tale Mazes is a new work, first published by Dover Publications, Inc., in 1997.

International Standard Book Number: 0-486-29547-8

Manufactured in the United States of America
Dover Publications, Inc., 31 East 2nd Street, Mineola, N.Y. 11501

Note

Inside this book you'll find 46 mazes featuring many of your favorite fairy tale characters. Each maze illustrates a different scene from a fairy tale; the characters won't be able to find the proper paths through the puzzles without your help.

Be sure to enter each maze where it says "START." After you have finished the puzzles, you can go back and color the pictures.

Solutions appear in the back of the book, beginning on page 53.

START

END

Find the path from the wicked queen to Snow White, whom the magic mirror chose as the fairest in the land.

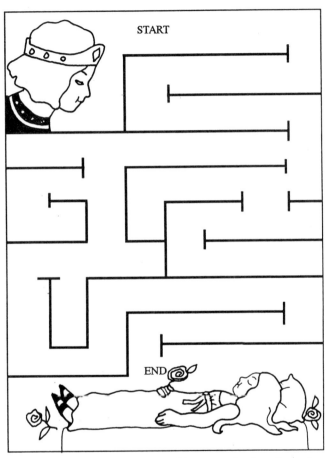

Help the prince find Snow White to wake her from her enchanted sleep.

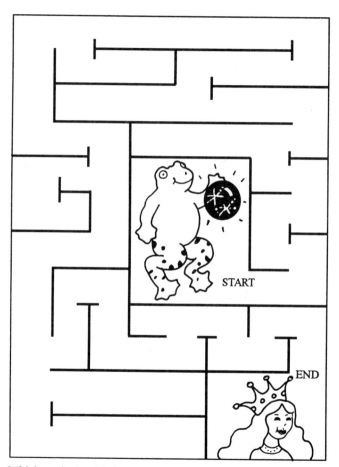

START

END

Which path should the Frog Prince take to return the golden ball to the princess?

START

END

Help Hansel and Gretel follow the right path to the witch's candy house.

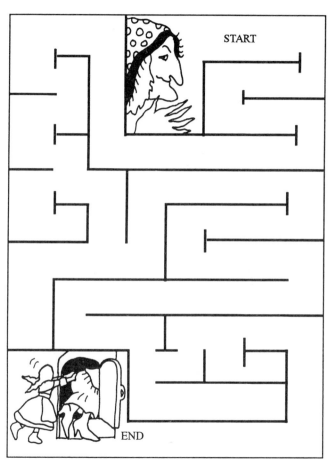

START

END

The witch has fattened up Hansel for dinner. Can you find out who actually gets pushed into the oven?

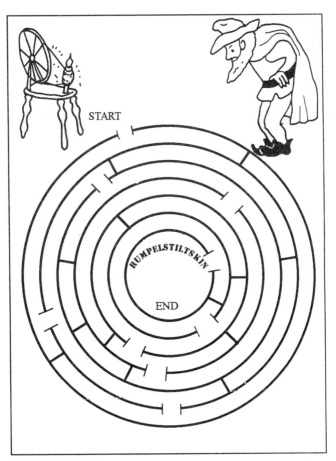

START

RUMPELSTILTSKIN

END

The queen must guess the dwarf's name to save her child.
Follow the correct path to discover what it is.
12

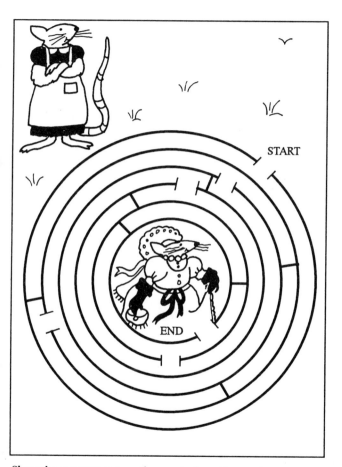

START

END

Show the country mouse the way to her city cousin.

START

END

Snow-white and Rose-red want to find their dear friend the bear. Show them where he is.

14

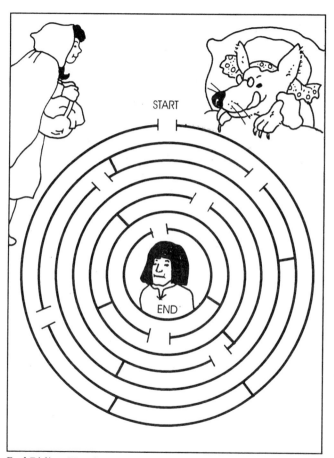

START

END

Red Riding Hood needs the woodsman's help to save her from the wolf. Find the correct path for her.

The soldier is trying to find the saucer-eyed dog that guards the magic tinder box.

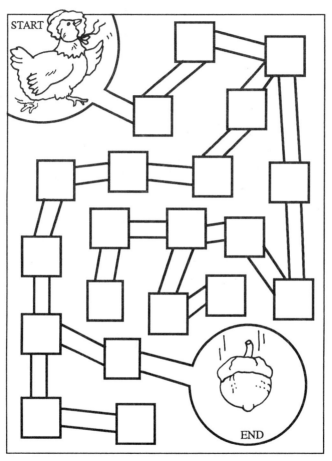

Something fell on Henny Penny's head. Can you find the correct path and discover what it was?

17

This rat from Hamelin must follow the Pied Piper. Which path will lead to him?

18

The children are being drawn to the Pied Piper's music. Show them the way.

19

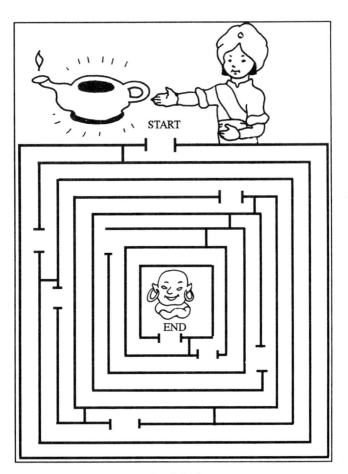

START

END

Help Aladdin find the genie of the lamp.

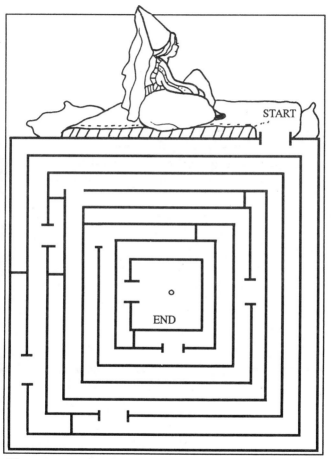

START

END

The princess can't sleep. Can you find the pea beneath her mattresses that is keeping her awake?

The donkey has decided to become a musician. Lead him to his friend the cat so that he can share the news.

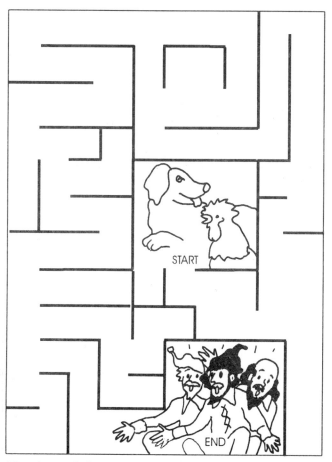

The dog and the rooster are going to join the cat and the donkey, but first they must frighten away the robbers.

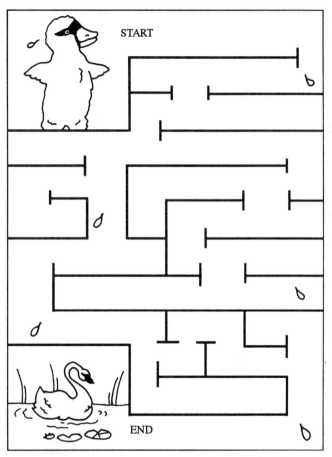

Follow the correct path to learn what the ugly duckling will become when it grows up.

24

The little boy sees that the emperor is wearing no clothes. Take him to the emperor to tell him the news.

Help the Little Red Hen reach the cake she made all by herself.

START

END

The Big Bad Wolf will find at the end of the path that the third little pig has built his house of bricks.

The Gingerbread Man is running away. How will he get to the stream that the fox pretends to help him cross?

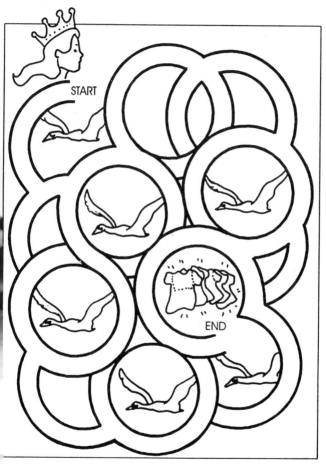

Lead the queen to the shirts that she sewed in order to turn the bewitched swans back into her brothers.

The tin soldier must escape from the water rat. Help him find his way.

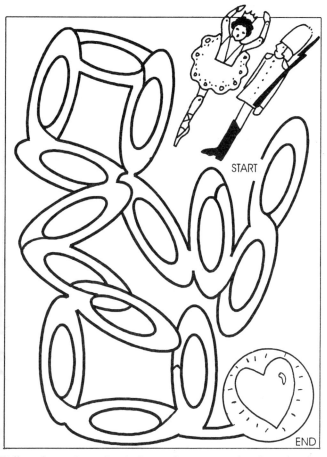

START

END

Follow the path to the tin heart that was made when the tin
soldier and the ballet dancer fell into the fire.

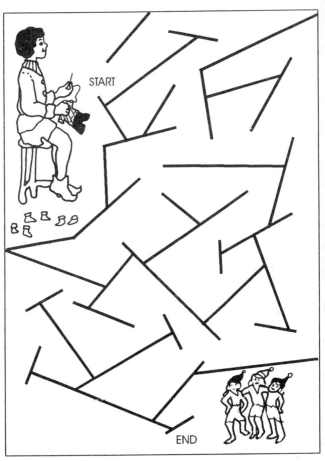

START

END

Where should the shoemaker leave the tiny clothes he sewed for the elves?

The prince must follow the path of Rapunzel's hair to climb her tower.

START

END

The king has ordered the Little Tailor to rid his kingdom of the giants. Where will he find them?

The Little Tailor must catch the unicorn to win the princess'
hand. Show him the correct path.

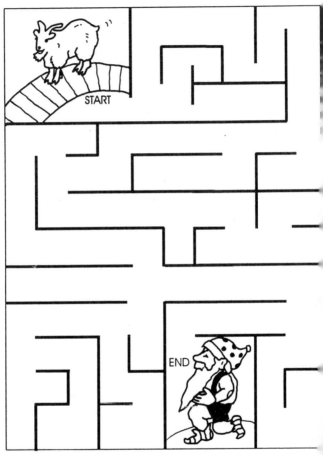

Help the Big Billy-Goat Gruff find the troll under the bridge so that he can scare him away.

36

Clever Elsa has gone to the cellar, where she worries about the
axe overhead. Help her father find her.

37

The baby bear would like to find out who is sitting in his chair.
Do you know who it is?

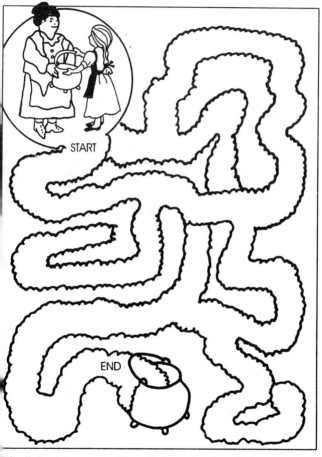

START

END

The little girl must say "Stop, little pot," to keep it from cooking more porridge. Lead her to the pot.

START

END

Follow the path to the maiden who laughed at the sight of Idle
Jack carrying a donkey on his back.

40

START

END

Find the path to the Snow Queen in her palace, where Gerda will search for her friend Kai.

41

START

END

Help Thumbelina fly to her tiny home in the big flower.

Follow the path from the worn-out shoes of the twelve dancing princesses to where the good witch is holding a magic cloak.

Tom Thumb has had many adventures. Now he's ready to return home and needs to find the correct path there.

44

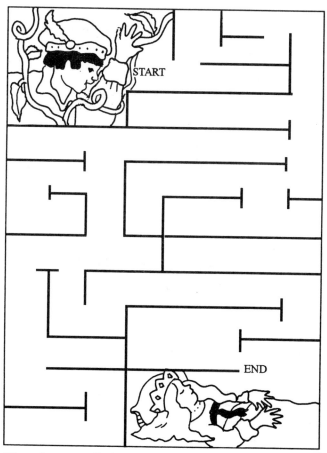

START

END

The prince must find his way into the castle to wake Sleeping
Beauty with a kiss.

Beauty sees in the magic mirror that the Beast is in trouble.
Help her find the path to him.

46

Lead the fairy to the poor man who wished a sausage onto the end of his wife's nose.

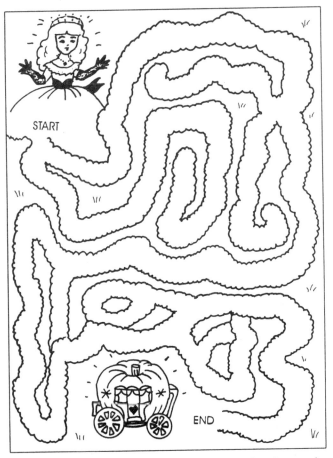

START

END

Take Cinderella to the coach that her fairy godmother made out of a pumpkin.

48

The prince needs to find Cinderella, in order to try the glass slipper on her foot.

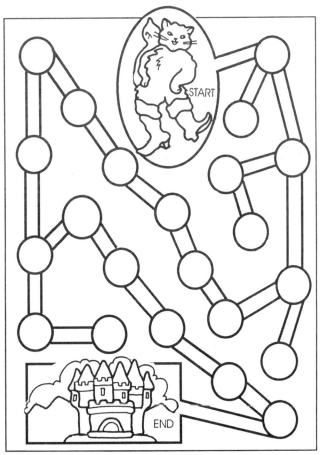

Puss in Boots would like to find the road that leads to the king's castle.

Follow the correct path down the beanstalk to discover who wants to steal the giant's golden hen.

START

GIVE ME MY BONE!

END

The Teeny-Tiny Woman in her bed hears a voice saying "Give me my bone!" Where is it coming from?

52

Solutions

page 7

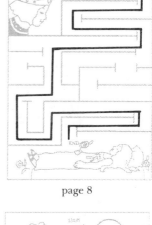

page 8

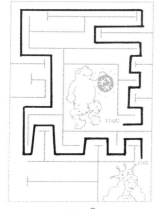

page 9

page 10

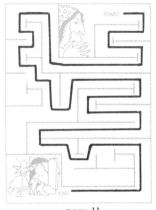

page 11

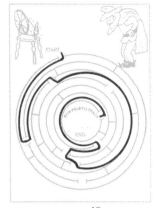

page 12

page 13

page 14

page 15

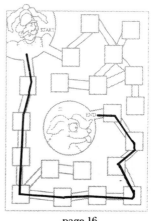

page 16

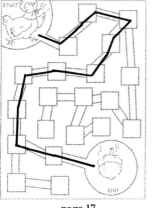

page 17

page 18

page 19

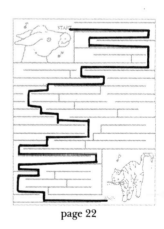

page 20

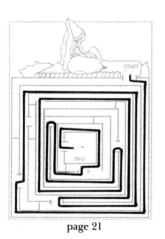

page 21

page 22

56

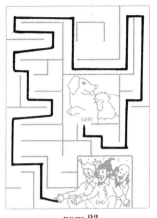

page 23

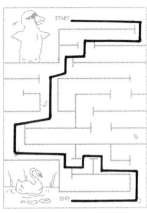

page 24

page 25

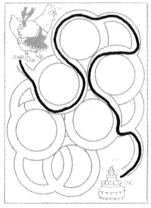

page 26

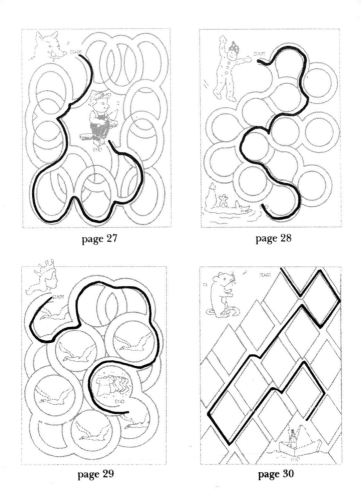

page 27

page 28

page 29

page 30

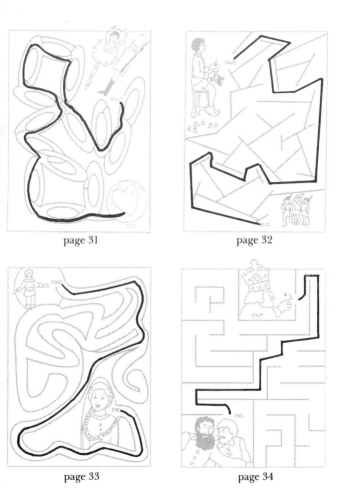

page 31

page 32

page 33

page 34

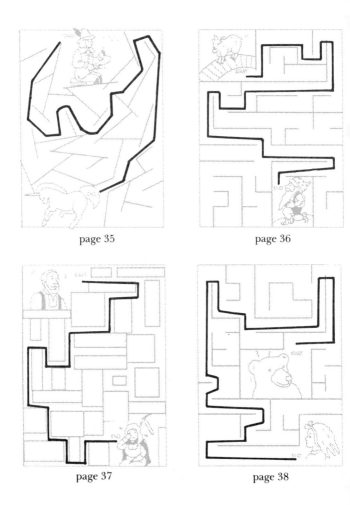

page 35

page 36

page 37

page 38

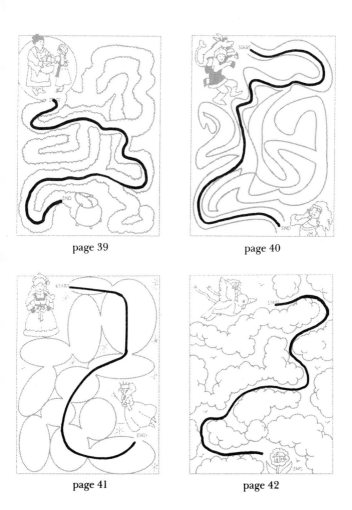

page 39

page 40

page 41

page 42

61

page 43

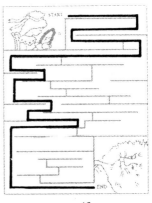

page 44

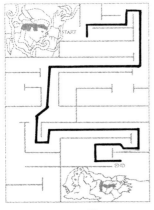

page 45

page 46

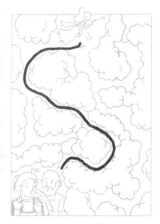

page 47

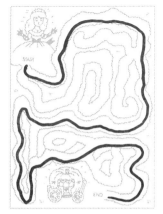

page 48

page 49

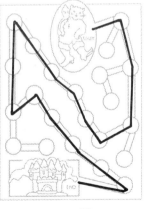

page 50

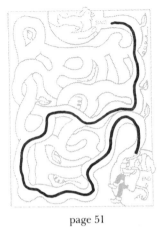

page 51

page 52